Silver Burdett Ginn
Mathematics

Practice Workbook

Cumulative Practice

Mixed Review

3

Silver Burdett Ginn

Parsippany, NJ

Atlanta, GA • Deerfield, IL • Irving, TX • Needham, MA • Upland, CA

Silver Burdett Ginn

1999 Printing

© 1998 Silver Burdett Ginn Inc. All rights reserved. Printed in the United States of America.
The publisher hereby grants permission to reproduce these pages in part or in whole, for
classroom use only.

ISBN 0-382-37290-5

13 –B- 02 01

Contents

Contents

Investigating Number Patterns

Write three addition or subtraction sentences
for each set. Write odd or even numbers.
Then, write if the sums or differences are odd or even.

1. ODD + ODD

____ + ____ = ____

____ + ____ = ____

____ + ____ = ____

The sums are _____.

2. EVEN + EVEN

____ + ____ = ____

____ + ____ = ____

____ + ____ = ____

The sums are _____.

3. ODD + EVEN

____ + ____ = ____

____ + ____ = ____

____ + ____ = ____

The sums are _____.

4. ODD – EVEN

____ – ____ = ____

____ – ____ = ____

____ – ____ = ____

The differences are _____.

5. EVEN – EVEN

____ – ____ = ____

____ – ____ = ____

____ – ____ = ____

The differences are _____.

6. ODD – ODD

____ – ____ = ____

____ – ____ = ____

____ – ____ = ____

The differences are _____.

Review and Remember

Add or subtract.

1. $9 - 8 =$ _____

2. $4 + 4 =$ _____

3. $12 - 6 =$ _____

4. $4 + 3 =$ _____

5. $8 + 7 =$ _____

6. $14 - 6 =$ _____

Rounding to the Nearest Ten and Hundred

Round to the nearest ten.

30 31 32 33 34 35 36 37 38 39 40

1. 32 ____   **2.** 35 ____   **3.** 38 ____

4. 34 ____   **5.** 36 ____   **6.** 31 ____

7. 45 ____   **8.** 53 ____   **9.** 71 ____

Round to the nearest ten. Circle the letter of the correct answer.

10. 57   **11.** 41   **12.** 75   **13.** 92

   a. 50   **a.** 30   **a.** 50   **a.** 80

   b. 60   **b.** 40   **b.** 70   **b.** 90

   c. 70   **c.** 50   **c.** 80   **c.** 100

Round to the nearest hundred.

300 310 320 330 340 350 360 370 380 390 400

14. 341 ____   **15.** 350 ____   **16.** 363 ____   **17.** 329 ____

18. 435 ____   **19.** 529 ____   **20.** 617 ____   **21.** 903 ____

Review and Remember

Add or subtract.

1.	**2.**	**3.**	**4.**	**5.**	**6.**
3	5	6	4	8	5
4	3	1	2	1	4
+4	+5	+8	+7	+1	+3

7.	**8.**	**9.**	**10.**	**11.**	**12.**
14	11	16	18	16	12
−2	−6	−2	−9	−8	−5

Reading and Writing Four-Digit Numbers

Write each number.

1. 2 thousands 4 hundreds 2 tens 5 ones _____

2. 6 thousands 1 hundred 0 tens 9 ones _____

3. 8 thousands 3 hundreds 4 tens 2 ones _____

4. 5 thousands 6 hundreds 9 tens 4 ones _____

5. 5,000 + 600 + 70 + 9 _____   **6.** 9,000 + 800 + 20 + 1 _____

7. 1,000 + 200 + 4 _____   **8.** 4,000 + 200 + 50 + 7 _____

Give the value of the digit 5.

9. 4,563   **10.** 5,014   **11.** 1,250   **12.** 6,745

_____   _____   _____   _____

Write the word name for each number.

13. 275 _____

14. 3,407 _____

15. 8,015 _____

Review and Remember

Add.

1. 5
     + 2

2. 3
     + 3

3. 2
     + 8

4. 9
     + 0

5. 3
     + 7

6. 4
     + 3

Write the numbers that come between.

7. 16 and 19   **8.** 27 and 32   **9.** 49 and 55

_____   _____   _____

Comparing and Ordering Numbers

Compare. Write > or < in each ◯.

1. 322 ◯ 321   **2.** 689 ◯ 3,869   **3.** 5,018 ◯ 5,118

4. 870 ◯ 6,087   **5.** 8,432 ◯ 4,823   **6.** 581 ◯ 381

7. 4,960 ◯ 4,962 **8.** 9,180 ◯ 8,190   **9.** 2,224 ◯ 2,325

Write the numbers in order from least to greatest.

10. 3,246 2,436 4,233   **11.** 6,198 3,427 7,866

_____ _____ _____   _____ _____ _____

12. 4,380 4,038 3,444   **13.** 1,326 3,621 6,140

_____ _____ _____   _____ _____ _____

14. 999   9   9,000   **15.** 4,022 8,042 2,048

_____ _____ _____   _____ _____ _____

16. 77   7   7,777   **17.** 3,906 9,063 6,039

_____ _____ _____   _____ _____ _____

Review and Remember

Add or subtract.

1. 8   **2.** 7   **3.** 8   **4.** 4   **5.** 2   **6.** 8
   + 9   + 5   + 8   + 9   + 9   + 4

7. 13   **8.** 12   **9.** 11   **10.** 11   **11.** 13   **12.** 12
   − 5   − 4   − 7   − 3   − 7   − 9

13. 9 + 8 = ____   **14.** 5 + 9 = ____   **15.** 8 + 4 = ____

16. 11 − 6 = ____   **17.** 13 − 9 = ____   **18.** 12 − 7 = ____

Name _____

Counting Coins and Bills

Write each value. Use a dollar sign and a decimal point.

1. forty-two cents _____

2. eighty-two cents _____

3. two dollars and twenty cents

_____

4. three dollars and sixty cents

_____

5. 3 dimes, 2 pennies

_____

6. 8 one-dollar bills, 4 dimes

_____

7. 6 one-dollar bills, 3 pennies

_____

8. 4 one-dollar bills, 1 dime

_____

9. 6 dimes, 8 pennies

_____

10. 5 one-dollar bills, 9 dimes

_____

Write the missing amount.

11. 3 one-dollar bills = _____ dimes

12. 6 quarters = _____ dimes

13. 3 one-dollar bills = _____ pennies

14. 6 quarters = _____ pennies

Review and Remember

Add or subtract.

1. 9
   + 9

2. 6
   + 8

3. 3
   + 9

4. 6
   + 9

5. 8
   + 7

6. 9
   + 7

7. 13
   − 4

8. 11
   − 2

9. 12
   − 5

10. 11
   − 6

11. 13
   − 8

12. 12
   − 4

13. 8
   + 8

14. 16
   − 7

15. 5
   + 7

16. 3
   + 6

17. 18
   − 6

18. 4
   + 3

Name _____

Using Addition Strategies

Add.

1. 6 +5	**2.** 7 +7	**3.** 8 +3	**4.** 8 +8	**5.** 6 +7
6. 5 +8	**7.** 6 +6	**8.** 7 +8	**9.** 9 +4	**10.** 9 +9
11. 9 +0	**12.** 8 +6	**13.** 5 +7	**14.** 9 +8	**15.** 0 +2

16. 7 + 6 = _____   **17.** 9 + 6 = _____   **18.** 4 + 8 = _____

19. 9 + 5 = _____   **20.** 1 + 6 = _____   **21.** 4 + 5 = _____

Find the output.

Rule: Add 9

	Input	Output
22.	3	
23.	7	
24.	5	
25.	8	

Rule: Add 3

	Input	Output
26.	12	
27.	6	
28.	4	
29.	9	

Review and Remember

Molly and Tom each made 4 potholders.
How many potholders did they make altogether?   _____

Adding Three Numbers

Add.

1. 3 2 +6	**2.** 7 0 +4	**3.** 5 4 +4	**4.** 4 1 +8	**5.** 5 4 +3

6. 7 2 +7	**7.** 7 1 +8	**8.** 6 1 +7	**9.** 8 0 +9	**10.** 2 3 +4

11. 5 0 +8	**12.** 4 4 +4	**13.** 2 2 +7	**14.** 1 0 +8	**15.** 7 2 +6

16. $6 + 0 + 9 =$ _____   **17.** $7 + 1 + 6 =$ _____   **18.** $4 + 4 + 3 =$ _____

Choose the correct sum. Circle the letter of your answer.

19. $6 + 3 + 4 =$ ☐   **a.** 13   **b.** 12   **c.** 14

20. $5 + 0 + 6 =$ ☐   **a.** 5   **b.** 16   **c.** 11

Review and Remember

Add.

1. 5 +4	**2.** 8 +1	**3.** 3 +7	**4.** 4 +3	**5.** 2 +8	**6.** 6 +3

7. 7 +1	**8.** 3 +6	**9.** 2 +6	**10.** 7 +5	**11.** 6 +3	**12.** 8 +3

Using Subtraction Strategies

Subtract.

1. 15 − 7	**2.** 9 − 0	**3.** 14 − 7	**4.** 15 − 9	**5.** 14 − 6
6. 17 − 9	**7.** 6 − 6	**8.** 13 − 4	**9.** 16 − 8	**10.** 14 − 5
11. 18 − 9	**12.** 15 − 8	**13.** 16 − 9	**14.** 14 − 9	**15.** 8 − 8

16. 14 − 8 = _____   **17.** 7 − 7 = _____   **18.** 13 − 4 = _____

19. 15 − 7 = _____   **20.** 17 − 8 = _____   **21.** 12 − 8 = _____

Solve.

22. There are 15 books and 8 children.
How many more books are there than children? _____ books

Review and Remember

Add or subtract. Use mental math or paper and pencil.

1. 3 1 + 1	**2.** 4 2 + 3	**3.** 3 0 + 3	**4.** 4 1 + 5	**5.** 2 3 + 3	**6.** 2 0 + 1
7. 10 − 4	**8.** 9 − 2	**9.** 9 − 8	**10.** 8 − 3	**11.** 10 − 3	**12.** 10 − 5

13. 7 − 1 = _____   **14.** 12 − 3 = _____   **15.** 9 − 5 = _____

16. 8 − 6 = _____   **17.** 7 + 7 = _____   **18.** 12 + 6 = _____

Name _____

Thinking Addition to Subtract

Find each missing addend. Then write each difference.

1.
```
    7          11
+  [ ]        − 7
  ─────       ────
   11
```

2.
```
    9          18
+  [ ]        − 9
  ─────       ────
   18
```

3.
```
    6           9
+  [ ]        − 6
  ─────       ────
    9
```

4.
```
    4          12
+  [ ]        − 4
  ─────       ────
   12
```

5.
```
    8          17
+  [ ]        − 8
  ─────       ────
   17
```

6.
```
    6           7
+  [ ]        − 6
  ─────       ────
    7
```

7.
```
    5          11
+  [ ]        − 5
  ─────       ────
   11
```

8.
```
    5          13
+  [ ]        − 5
  ─────       ────
   13
```

9. $9 + [\ ] = 13$

   $13 − 9 = $ _____

10. $6 + [\ ] = 10$

   $10 − 6 = $ _____

11. $6 + [\ ] = 12$

   $12 − 6 = $ _____

12. $4 + [\ ] = 13$

   $13 − 4 = $ _____

Review and Remember

Add or subtract.

1.
```
   3
 + 4
 ────
```
2.
```
   4
 + 4
 ────
```
3.
```
   3
 + 7
 ────
```
4.
```
   5
 + 0
 ────
```
5.
```
   8
 + 2
 ────
```
6.
```
   7
 + 1
 ────
```

7.
```
   7
 − 1
 ────
```
8.
```
  10
 − 2
 ────
```
9.
```
   5
 − 1
 ────
```
10.
```
   9
 − 6
 ────
```
11.
```
   9
 − 2
 ────
```
12.
```
   6
 − 4
 ────
```

Families of Facts

Complete each fact family.

1. 8 + 7 = _____

    7 + 8 = _____

    15 − 7 = _____

    15 − 8 = _____

2. 6 + 8 = _____

    8 + 6 = _____

    14 − 6 = _____

    14 − 8 = _____

3. 9 + 7 = _____

    7 + 9 = _____

    16 − 7 = _____

    16 − 9 = _____

4. 9 + 3 = _____

    3 + 9 = _____

    12 − 3 = _____

    12 − 9 = _____

5. 7 + 6 = _____

    6 + 7 = _____

    13 − 6 = _____

    13 − 7 = _____

6. 5 + 9 = _____

    9 + 5 = _____

    14 − 5 = _____

    14 − 9 = _____

Write a fact family for each.

7. | 4, 5, 9 |

8. | 8, 4, 12 |

_____ _____ _____ _____

_____ _____ _____ _____

Review and Remember

Add or subtract.

1. 7 + 6 = _____

2. 5 + 8 = _____

3. 6 + 9 = _____

4. 11 − 2 = _____

5. 15 − 9 = _____

6. 12 − 6 = _____

Compare. Write >, <, or = in each ◯.

7. 8 + 2 ◯ 11 − 1

8. 6 + 7 ◯ 4 + 8

9. 15 − 4 ◯ 5 + 7

10. 16 − 6 ◯ 7 + 4

Adding Greater Numbers

Add. For 1–16, check by adding up.

1. 522
    + 747

2. 645
    + 391

3. 927
    + 739

4. 788
    + 935

5.   28
     469
    + 583

6. 595
     414
    + 107

7. 667
     684
    + 729

8. 145
     783
    + 229

9. 6,894
    + 8,796

10. 9,678
     + 4,983

11. 6,825
     + 5,549

12. 5,634
     + 8,365

13. 9,843
     + 5,045

14. 6,945
     + 6,812

15. 7,648
     + 8,579

16. 6,543
     + 7,432

17. 7,983 + 6,748 ———

18. 6,167 + 7,709 ———

19. 8,074 + 725 ———

20. 9,287 + 8,948 ———

Review and Remember

Round each number to the nearest ten.

1. 37 ———

2. 41 ———

3. 65 ———

4. 78 ———

Add. Use mental math or paper and pencil.

5. 45
    + 42

6. 37
    + 25

7. 82
    + 11

8. 54
    + 33

9. 49
    + 32

10. 77
     + 18

Estimating Differences

Round to the nearest ten and estimate each difference.

1. 27
  − 12

2. 34
  − 15

3. 62
  − 29

4. 65
  − 55

Round to the nearest hundred and estimate each difference.

5. 354
  − 217

6. 716
  − 280

7. 663
  − 450

8. 749
  − 552

9. 650
  − 350

10. 352
  − 176

11. 322
  − 101

12. 682
  − 552

Compare. Write >, <, or = in each ⬭.

Choose estimation, paper and pencil, or a calculator.

13. 52 − 14 ⬭ 75 − 47

14. 72 − 18 ⬭ 42 − 13

15. 63 − 32 ⬭ 68 − 21

16. 43 − 37 ⬭ 29 − 17

Review and Remember

Give the value of the digit 6.

1. 56,125

2. 612,975

3. 41,675

_____

_____

_____

Give the value.

4.

_____

Subtracting Two- and Three-Digit Numbers

Subtract. Check by adding.

	tens	ones
1.	7	3
	− 2	1

	tens	ones
2.	6	5
	− 4	2

	tens	ones
3.	8	9
	− 2	3

4. 40
  − 20

5. 48
  − 32

6. 67
  − 12

7. 42
  − 31

8. 46
  − 5

9. 35
  − 22

10. 49
  − 13

11. 53
  − 20

12. 285
  − 134

13. 471
  − 248

14. 750
  − 325

15. 803
  − 502

16. 438
  − 263

17. 839
  − 570

18. 217
  − 93

19. 504
  − 484

Review and Remember

Add or subtract.

1. 32
  + 14

2. 38
  + 13

3. 25
  + 11

4. 26
  + 36

5. 15
  + 23

6. 9
  − 5

7. 7
  − 2

8. 8
  − 3

9. 5
  − 4

10. 6
  − 2

11. 19 + 23 _____

12. 16 + 20 _____

13. 18 + 32 _____

Use after Grade 3, text page 107. **13**

Subtracting Greater Numbers

Subtract. Check by adding.

1. 8,769 − 6,548	**2.** 7,695 − 5,456	**3.** 8,740 − 2,270	**4.** 6,875 − 5,769
5. 7,824 − 3,089	**6.** 9,536 − 6,287	**7.** 9,924 − 5,447	**8.** 6,943 − 2,678
9. 8,521 − 6,339	**10.** 6,105 − 1,876	**11.** 3,001 − 1,246	**12.** 8,240 − 2,683

13. 4,117 − 1,238 _____

14. 7,143 − 3,864 _____

Solve.

15. The odometer on Mr. Brown's car reads 7,148 miles. It read 5,795 miles three months ago. How far did Mr. Brown drive in three months?

_____

16. The odometer on Mrs. O'Key's car reads 9,206 miles. It read 6,789 miles two months ago. How far did Mrs. O'Key drive in two months?

_____

Review and Remember

Add or subtract.

1. 35 42 + 37	**2.** 68 31 + 25	**3.** 73 64 + 89	**4.** 38 47 + 65	**5.** 22 37 + 63	**6.** 91 27 + 36
7. 12 − 6	**8.** 11 − 3	**9.** 12 − 7	**10.** 13 − 9	**11.** 11 − 2	**12.** 13 − 5

Subtracting Across Zeros

Subtract. Estimate to be sure your answers make sense.

1. 600
  − 563

2. 805
  − 284

3. 400
  − 289

4. 602
  − 474

5. 704
  − 386

6. 800
  − 659

7. 402
  − 125

8. 702
  − 196

9. 405 − 88 = _____

10. 502 − 193 = _____

11. 300 − 284 = _____

12. 207 − 128 = _____

Find the correct difference. Choose mental math
or paper and pencil. Circle your answer.

13. 807 − 208
  a. 599
  b. 699
  c. 601

14. 250 − 117
  a. 143
  b. 133
  c. 147

15. 600 − 256
  a. 456
  b. 353
  c. 344

16. 300 − 197
  a. 203
  b. 103
  c. 113

17. 540 − 206
  a. 236
  b. 346
  c. 334

18. 907 − 259
  a. 656
  b. 752
  c. 648

Review and Remember

Compare. Write >, <, or = in each ⬭.

1. 1,742 ◯ 1,724

2. 6,127 ◯ 6,227

3. 3,110 ◯ 3,101

4. 4,223 ◯ 4,223

Use estimation to choose the letter of the correct answer.
Circle your answer.

5. 592 + 215   **a.** 707   **b.** 383   **c.** 807

Elapsed Time

Write each time in two ways.

1.

_____

_____

2.

_____

_____

3.

_____

_____

Write what time it will be:

4. in 3 hours.

11:00

_____

5. in 2 hours.

9:00

_____

6. in 20 minutes.

2:20

_____

About how long does it take? Choose *a* or *b*.

7. drinking milk	**a.** 5 hours	**b.** 5 minutes
8. making a phone call	**a.** 10 minutes	**b.** 10 hours
9. taking a nap	**a.** 2 hours	**b.** 2 minutes
10. taking a walk	**a.** 20 minutes	**b.** 20 hours

Review and Remember

Add.

1. 4,786	**2.** 3,747	**3.** 4,921	**4.** 5,783
+ 2,894	+ 1,386	+ 5,382	+ 1,207

5. $0.15 + $0.25 = _____

6. $0.72 + $0.21 = _____

Name _____

Using Customary Units of Length and Capacity

Choose *in., ft, yd,* or *mi* to measure each length.

1. length of a hallway _____

2. distance from Ohio to Boston _____

3. width of the classroom _____

4. width of a notebook _____

Complete.

5. 1 ft = _____ in.

6. 36 in. = _____ yd

7. 3 yd = _____ ft

8. 24 in. = _____ ft

Choose *cup, pint, quart,* or *gallon* to measure each amount.

9. a bathtub full of water _____

10. orange juice for 2 people _____

11. glass of milk _____

12. fish tank of water _____

13. pitcher of milk _____

14. hot cocoa for 1 person _____

Choose the better estimate for each.

15. a bucket of water

    a. 3 gallons   **b.** 3 pints

16. a tank full of gasoline

    a. 4 gallons   **b.** 14 gallons

17. yogurt for lunch

    a. 1 quart   **b.** 1 cup

18. soup for 4 people

    a. 2 pints   **b.** 2 gallons

Review and Remember

Add or subtract.

1. 235
  + 141

2. 342
  + 451

3. 621
  + 143

4. 340
  + 127

5. 470
  − 143

6. 593
  − 24

7. 429
  − 170

8. 362
  − 238

Using Metric Units of Length and Capacity

Choose *cm, m,* or *km* to complete each sentence.

1. The distance from St. Louis to Chicago is about 540 _____.

2. A large paper clip is about 4 _____ long.

3. A pencil is about 14 _____ long.

4. The length of the school cafeteria is about 17 _____ .

Complete.

5. 1,000 m = _____ km

6. 1 m = _____ cm

7. 100 cm = _____ m

8. 2 km = _____ m

Choose *milliliter* or *liter* to measure the capacity of each item.

9. tank of oil _____

10. pitcher of milk _____

11. pot of water _____

12. teaspoon of gravy _____

13. glass of juice _____

14. raindrop _____

Choose the best estimate for each.

15. a glass of milk

   a. 150 L   **b.** 150 mL

   c. 500 mL   **d.** 5 mL

16. a bowl of soup

   a. 300 mL   **b.** 30 mL

   c. 300 L   **d.** 3 L

Review and Remember

Add or subtract.

1. 341
+ 232

2. 172
+ 413

3. 300
+ 161

4. 401
+ 183

5. 310
− 140

6. 701
− 451

7. 600
− 361

8. 810
− 643

Name _____

Ounces and Pounds, Grams and Kilograms

Choose *ounce* or *pound* to measure how heavy each item is.

1. a dog _____   **2.** a pencil _____

3. a paper airplane _____   **4.** a bear _____

5. an eraser _____   **6.** a dictionary _____

Choose the better estimate for each.

7. a car   **8.** one apple

    a. 3,000 pounds   **b.** 30 pounds   **a.** 5 ounces   **b.** 5 pounds

Choose *gram* or *kilogram* to measure how heavy each item is.

9. a bag of grain _____   **10.** a marble _____

11. a feather _____   **12.** a watermelon _____

13. a watch _____   **14.** a leaf _____

Compare. Write >, <, or = in each ◯.

15. 2 g ◯ 2 kg   **16.** 8 g ◯ 1 kg   **17.** 2,000 g ◯ 2 kg

18. 3,000 g ◯ 1 kg   **19.** 5 g ◯ 5 kg   **20.** 1,000 g ◯ 1 kg

21. 10 g ◯ 2 g   **22.** 100 g ◯ 100 kg   **23.** 3 kg ◯ 300 g

Review and Remember

Round each number to the nearest ten.

1. 61 _____   **2.** 26 _____   **3.** 43 _____   **4.** 89 _____

Add. Use mental math or paper and pencil.

5.	**6.**	**7.**	**8.**	**9.**	**10.**
33	21	65	48	17	59
+ 27	+ 73	+ 28	+ 39	+ 55	+ 32

Name _____

Reading a Thermometer

Write each Fahrenheit temperature shown.

1.  **2.**  **3.**  **4.**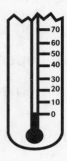

_____   _____   _____   _____

Write each Celsius temperature shown. Circle the answer that is closest to the temperature at which water freezes.

5. 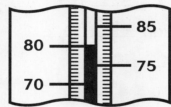 **6.** 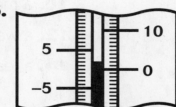 **7.**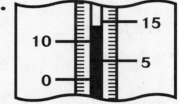

_____   _____   _____

Review and Remember

Add or subtract. Use mental math or paper and pencil.

1. $\begin{array}{r}3\\3\\+7\\\hline\end{array}$	**2.** $\begin{array}{r}4\\4\\+5\\\hline\end{array}$	**3.** $\begin{array}{r}7\\0\\+8\\\hline\end{array}$	**4.** $\begin{array}{r}9\\0\\+8\\\hline\end{array}$	**5.** $\begin{array}{r}5\\2\\+9\\\hline\end{array}$	**6.** $\begin{array}{r}2\\8\\+6\\\hline\end{array}$
7. $\begin{array}{r}17\\-8\\\hline\end{array}$	**8.** $\begin{array}{r}15\\-7\\\hline\end{array}$	**9.** $\begin{array}{r}15\\-9\\\hline\end{array}$	**10.** $\begin{array}{r}16\\-8\\\hline\end{array}$	**11.** $\begin{array}{r}18\\-9\\\hline\end{array}$	**12.** $\begin{array}{r}16\\-7\\\hline\end{array}$

13. $14 - 6 =$ _____   **14.** $14 - 7 =$ _____   **15.** $17 - 2 =$ _____

Name _____

Understanding Multiplication

Solve.

1. 2 + 2 + 2 = _____

How many 2s? _____

_____ 2s = _____

2. 3 + 3 + 3 = _____

How many 3s? _____

_____ 3s = _____

3. 4 + 4 + 4 + 4 = _____

4 × 4 = _____

4. 5 + 5 = _____

2 × 5 = _____

5. 9 + 9 = _____

2 × 9 = _____

6. 6 + 6 + 6 = _____

3 × 6 = _____

7. 5 + 5 + 5 = _____

3 × 5 = _____

8. 7 + 7 = _____

2 × 7 = _____

9. 2 + 2 + 2 + 2 = _____

4 × 2 = _____

10. 4 + 4 + 4 = _____

3 × 4 = _____

11. 3 + 3 + 3 + 3 = _____

4 × 3 = _____

12. 7 + 7 + 7 = _____

3 × 7 = _____

Review and Remember

Tell what time it will be in 3 hours.

1. 7:00 _____

2. 10:30 _____

Use the sign to answer.

3. Suppose it is 10:30. Can Jim eat
lunch in the cafeteria?

_____

CAFETERIA
OPEN FOR LUNCH
FROM 11:00 – 2:00

Use after Grade 3, text page 177. **21**

Name _____

Using 2 and 3 as Factors

Find each product.

1. $\begin{array}{r} 4 \\ \times\ 2 \\ \hline \end{array}$
2. $\begin{array}{r} 2 \\ \times\ 1 \\ \hline \end{array}$
3. $\begin{array}{r} 6 \\ \times\ 2 \\ \hline \end{array}$
4. $\begin{array}{r} 2 \\ \times\ 3 \\ \hline \end{array}$
5. $\begin{array}{r} 5 \\ \times\ 2 \\ \hline \end{array}$

6. $\begin{array}{r} 2 \\ \times\ 2 \\ \hline \end{array}$
7. $\begin{array}{r} 7 \\ \times\ 2 \\ \hline \end{array}$
8. $\begin{array}{r} 9 \\ \times\ 2 \\ \hline \end{array}$
9. $\begin{array}{r} 2 \\ \times\ 4 \\ \hline \end{array}$
10. $\begin{array}{r} 2 \\ \times\ 3 \\ \hline \end{array}$

11. $\begin{array}{r} 3 \\ \times\ 3 \\ \hline \end{array}$
12. $\begin{array}{r} 6 \\ \times\ 3 \\ \hline \end{array}$
13. $\begin{array}{r} 3 \\ \times\ 5 \\ \hline \end{array}$
14. $\begin{array}{r} 7 \\ \times\ 3 \\ \hline \end{array}$
15. $\begin{array}{r} 3 \\ \times\ 8 \\ \hline \end{array}$

16. $3 \times 7 =$ _____
17. $3 \times 9 =$ _____
18. $3 \times 4 =$ _____

19. $8 \times 3 =$ _____
20. $9 \times 2 =$ _____
21. $7 \times 3 =$ _____

22. $6 \times 2 =$ _____
23. $9 \times 3 =$ _____
24. $5 \times 2 =$ _____

Solve.

25. There were 7 stools. Each stool had 3 legs. How many legs were there in all?

_____

26. There were 6 boys. Each boy had 2 toy cars. How many cars were there in all?

_____

Review and Remember

Add or subtract.

1. $\begin{array}{r} 6 \\ +\ 7 \\ \hline \end{array}$
2. $\begin{array}{r} 9 \\ +\ 9 \\ \hline \end{array}$
3. $\begin{array}{r} 8 \\ +\ 7 \\ \hline \end{array}$
4. $\begin{array}{r} 8 \\ +\ 9 \\ \hline \end{array}$
5. $\begin{array}{r} 6 \\ +\ 5 \\ \hline \end{array}$
6. $\begin{array}{r} 8 \\ +\ 8 \\ \hline \end{array}$

7. $\begin{array}{r} 34 \\ -\ 19 \\ \hline \end{array}$
8. $\begin{array}{r} 63 \\ -\ 28 \\ \hline \end{array}$
9. $\begin{array}{r} 72 \\ -\ 53 \\ \hline \end{array}$
10. $\begin{array}{r} 80 \\ -\ 43 \\ \hline \end{array}$
11. $\begin{array}{r} 58 \\ -\ 29 \\ \hline \end{array}$
12. $\begin{array}{r} 63 \\ -\ 39 \\ \hline \end{array}$

Using 4 and 5 as Factors

Find each product.

1. $\begin{array}{r} 4 \\ \times\, 2 \\ \hline \end{array}$
2. $\begin{array}{r} 4 \\ \times\, 4 \\ \hline \end{array}$
3. $\begin{array}{r} 5 \\ \times\, 7 \\ \hline \end{array}$
4. $\begin{array}{r} 4 \\ \times\, 1 \\ \hline \end{array}$
5. $\begin{array}{r} 5 \\ \times\, 3 \\ \hline \end{array}$

6. $\begin{array}{r} 4 \\ \times\, 5 \\ \hline \end{array}$
7. $\begin{array}{r} 9 \\ \times\, 4 \\ \hline \end{array}$
8. $\begin{array}{r} 6 \\ \times\, 5 \\ \hline \end{array}$
9. $\begin{array}{r} 4 \\ \times\, 4 \\ \hline \end{array}$
10. $\begin{array}{r} 8 \\ \times\, 5 \\ \hline \end{array}$

11. $\begin{array}{r} 6 \\ \times\, 4 \\ \hline \end{array}$
12. $\begin{array}{r} 1 \\ \times\, 5 \\ \hline \end{array}$
13. $\begin{array}{r} 0 \\ \times\, 4 \\ \hline \end{array}$
14. $\begin{array}{r} 5 \\ \times\, 9 \\ \hline \end{array}$
15. $\begin{array}{r} 0 \\ \times\, 5 \\ \hline \end{array}$

16. $7 \times 4 =$ _____

17. $9 \times 5 =$ _____

18. $7 \times 5 =$ _____

19. $8 \times 4 =$ _____

20. $5 \times 4 =$ _____

21. $6 \times 5 =$ _____

22. $5 \times 5 =$ _____

23. $4 \times 3 =$ _____

24. $2 \times 5 =$ _____

Solve.

25. Kim has 5 pages of pictures.
She has 4 pictures on each page.
How many pictures does Kim have? _____

Review and Remember

Round each number to the nearest ten.

1. 35 _____
2. 21 _____
3. 42 _____
4. 57_____

Round each number to the nearest hundred.

5. 111 _____
6. 217 _____
7. 481 _____
8. 154 _____

Using 0 Through 5 as Factors

Find each product.

1. $\begin{array}{r} 3 \\ \times 3 \\ \hline \end{array}$
2. $\begin{array}{r} 4 \\ \times 3 \\ \hline \end{array}$
3. $\begin{array}{r} 3 \\ \times 4 \\ \hline \end{array}$
4. $\begin{array}{r} 5 \\ \times 2 \\ \hline \end{array}$
5. $\begin{array}{r} 4 \\ \times 2 \\ \hline \end{array}$

6. $\begin{array}{r} 4 \\ \times 0 \\ \hline \end{array}$
7. $\begin{array}{r} 5 \\ \times 3 \\ \hline \end{array}$
8. $\begin{array}{r} 2 \\ \times 7 \\ \hline \end{array}$
9. $\begin{array}{r} 3 \\ \times 6 \\ \hline \end{array}$
10. $\begin{array}{r} 4 \\ \times 4 \\ \hline \end{array}$

11. $\begin{array}{r} 4 \\ \times 8 \\ \hline \end{array}$
12. $\begin{array}{r} 6 \\ \times 4 \\ \hline \end{array}$
13. $\begin{array}{r} 1 \\ \times 8 \\ \hline \end{array}$
14. $\begin{array}{r} 7 \\ \times 5 \\ \hline \end{array}$
15. $\begin{array}{r} 3 \\ \times 9 \\ \hline \end{array}$

16. $1 \times 2 = $ _____
17. $3 \times 2 = $ _____
18. $1 \times 6 = $ _____

19. $5 \times 4 = $ _____
20. $3 \times 7 = $ _____
21. $8 \times 0 = $ _____

22. $4 \times 2 = $ _____
23. $5 \times 5 = $ _____
24. $0 \times 1 = $ _____

Solve.

25. Bill has 6 boxes. He has 4 rocks in each box. How many rocks does Bill have? _____

Review and Remember

Tell what time it will be in 4 hours.

1. 3:45 _____
2. 9:15 _____
3. 11:00 _____

Add.

4. $3 + 5 + 8 = $ _____
5. $2 + 6 + 7 = $ _____

6. $21 + 13 + 16 = $ _____
7. $12 + 42 + 23 = $ _____

Using More Patterns to Multiply

Multiply.

1. 2 × 2 = _____

2 × 3 = _____

2 × 4 = _____

2 × 5 = _____

2. 4 × 2 = _____

4 × 3 = _____

4 × 4 = _____

4 × 5 = _____

3. 5 × 2 = _____

5 × 3 = _____

5 × 4 = _____

5 × 5 = _____

4. 3 × 7 = _____

3 × 8 = _____

3 × 9 = _____

5. 7 × 7 = _____

7 × 8 = _____

7 × 9 = _____

6. 9 × 7 = _____

9 × 8 = _____

9 × 9 = _____

7. 2 × 9 = _____

9 × 2 = _____

8. 4 × 3 = _____

3 × 4 = _____

9. 2 × 6 = _____

6 × 2 = _____

10. 3 × 8 = _____

8 × 3 = _____

11. 5 × 6 = _____

6 × 5 = _____

12. 4 × 8 = _____

8 × 4 = _____

13. 4 × 7 = _____

7 × 4 = _____

14. 5 × 8 = _____

8 × 5 = _____

15. 6 × 7 = _____

7 × 6 = _____

Review and Remember

Add.

1. 5 + 5 + 5 = _____

2. 4 + 4 + 4 = _____

3.   2,375
      +   156

4.   4,271
      +   327

5.   6,412
      +   539

6.   4,162
      + 3,475

7.   1,498
      + 8,364

8.   5,055
      + 2,407

Using 6 as a Factor

Find each product.

1.	6 $\times 3$	2.	4 $\times 6$	3.	2 $\times 6$	4.	6 $\times 5$	5.	6 $\times 1$

6.	6 $\times 7$	7.	5 $\times 6$	8.	9 $\times 6$	9.	6 $\times 8$	10.	0 $\times 6$

11. $6 \times 2 = $ _____   **12.** $7 \times 6 = $ _____   **13.** $1 \times 6 = $ _____

14. _____ $= 4 \times 6$ **15.** _____ $= 6 \times 6$ **16.** _____ $= 8 \times 6$

17. $6 \times 3 = $ _____   **18.** $6 \times 2 = $ _____   **19.** $9 \times 6 = $ _____

Solve.

20. Lyla pasted 5 pictures on each poster. She has
6 posters. How many pictures does Lyla have?   _____

21. Terry has 6 plants. He put 3 drops of plant
food in each pot. How many drops of plant
food did he use?   _____

Review and Remember

Add or subtract. Use mental math or paper and pencil.

1.	6 2 $+ 3$	2.	5 1 $+ 8$	3.	6 0 $+ 7$	4.	2 4 $+ 5$	5.	5 4 $+ 1$	6.	9 0 $+ 5$

7.	621 $- 189$	8.	333 $- 145$	9.	412 $- 143$	10.	622 $- 153$	11.	294 $- 187$	12.	721 $- 539$

Using 7 and 8 as Factors

Find each product.

1. $\begin{array}{r} 7 \\ \times\,3 \\ \hline \end{array}$	**2.** $\begin{array}{r} 8 \\ \times\,2 \\ \hline \end{array}$	**3.** $\begin{array}{r} 6 \\ \times\,7 \\ \hline \end{array}$	**4.** $\begin{array}{r} 8 \\ \times\,4 \\ \hline \end{array}$	**5.** $\begin{array}{r} 3 \\ \times\,8 \\ \hline \end{array}$
6. $\begin{array}{r} 8 \\ \times\,7 \\ \hline \end{array}$	**7.** $\begin{array}{r} 8 \\ \times\,8 \\ \hline \end{array}$	**8.** $\begin{array}{r} 5 \\ \times\,7 \\ \hline \end{array}$	**9.** $\begin{array}{r} 6 \\ \times\,8 \\ \hline \end{array}$	**10.** $\begin{array}{r} 7 \\ \times\,7 \\ \hline \end{array}$

11. $8 \times 0 =$ _____   **12.** $7 \times 4 =$ _____   **13.** $5 \times 8 =$ _____

14. _____ $= 8 \times 4$ **15.** _____ $= 7 \times 9$ **16.** _____ $= 2 \times 7$

Solve.

17. Patti made 4 necklaces. She used 8 beads for each. How many beads did Patti use? _____

18. Ken rode his bike 2 miles every day. How far did he ride in 7 days? _____

Review and Remember

Add or subtract.

1. $\begin{array}{r} 1{,}845 \\ +\ 3{,}569 \\ \hline \end{array}$	**2.** $\begin{array}{r} 3{,}769 \\ +\ 2{,}483 \\ \hline \end{array}$	**3.** $\begin{array}{r} 2{,}764 \\ +\ 4{,}453 \\ \hline \end{array}$	**4.** $\begin{array}{r} 3{,}107 \\ +\ 4{,}200 \\ \hline \end{array}$
5. $\begin{array}{r} 5{,}312 \\ +\ 2{,}418 \\ \hline \end{array}$	**6.** $\begin{array}{r} 1{,}810 \\ +\ 6{,}204 \\ \hline \end{array}$	**7.** $\begin{array}{r} 600 \\ -\ 229 \\ \hline \end{array}$	**8.** $\begin{array}{r} 800 \\ -\ 347 \\ \hline \end{array}$
9. $\begin{array}{r} 203 \\ -\ 117 \\ \hline \end{array}$	**10.** $\begin{array}{r} 408 \\ -\ 169 \\ \hline \end{array}$	**11.** $\begin{array}{r} 300 \\ -\ 148 \\ \hline \end{array}$	**12.** $\begin{array}{r} 700 \\ -\ 613 \\ \hline \end{array}$

Using 9 as a Factor

Find each product.

1. 9
    × 3

2. 9
    × 2

3. 6
    × 9

4. 9
    × 4

5. 3
    × 9

6. 9
    × 7

7. 9
    × 8

8. 5
    × 9

9. 4
    × 9

10. 9
    × 9

11. $9 \times 0 =$ _____

12. $9 \times 4 =$ _____

13. $5 \times 9 =$ _____

14. _____ $= 3 \times 9$

15. _____ $= 9 \times 1$

16. _____ $= 9 \times 6$

Solve.

17. Chad has 9 model planes on each shelf in his room. He has 3 shelves. How many model planes does Chad have? _____

18. Karen put 4 pumpkin seeds in each hole. She had dug 9 holes. How many pumpkin seeds did she plant? _____

Review and Remember

Add or subtract.

1. 84
    + 76

2. 793
    + 201

3. 483
    + 212

4. 86
    + 29

5. 348
    + 929

6. 438
    − 129

7. 614
    − 289

8. 98
    − 47

9. $942 - 611 =$ _____

10. $764 - 531 =$ _____

11. $379 - 163 =$ _____

Name _____

Multiplying Three Numbers

Multiply.

1. $2 \times 2 \times 3 =$ _____ **2.** $3 \times 2 \times 1 =$ _____

3. $7 \times 0 \times 4 =$ _____ **4.** $5 \times 1 \times 4 =$ _____

5. $4 \times 1 \times 8 =$ _____ **6.** $3 \times 4 \times 1 =$ _____

7. $7 \times 1 \times 8 =$ _____ **8.** $8 \times 0 \times 9 =$ _____

9. $3 \times 1 \times 8 =$ _____ **10.** $2 \times 3 \times 1 =$ _____

11. $5 \times 4 \times 1 =$ _____ **12.** $3 \times 2 \times 4 =$ _____

13. $2 \times 2 \times 4 =$ _____ **14.** $2 \times 3 \times 2 =$ _____

15. $2 \times 3 \times 3 =$ _____ **16.** $4 \times 1 \times 2 =$ _____

17. $2 \times 4 \times 2 =$ _____ **18.** $5 \times 1 \times 3 =$ _____

19. $6 \times 9 \times 0 =$ _____ **20.** $4 \times 2 \times 8 =$ _____

Review and Remember

Add or subtract. Use mental math or paper and pencil.

1.	**2.**	**3.**	**4.**	**5.**	**6.**
3	1	8	5	4	3
5	8	6	5	4	2
+ 4	+ 1	+ 1	+ 2	+ 3	+ 5

7.	**8.**	**9.**	**10.**
961	887	745	268
− 479	− 635	− 378	− 194

Finding Facts from Pictures

Use the picture to answer each question.

1. How many apples are there? _____

2. How many peaches are there? _____

3. How many lemons are there? _____

4. How many pumpkins and peaches are there? _____

5. How many lemons and peaches are there? _____

6. Are there more lemons or more apples? _____

7. Mark bought 4 pumpkins. How many are left? _____

Review and Remember

Add or subtract.

1.
```
   5
   2
 + 7
```

2.
```
   6
   1
 + 8
```

3.
```
   3
   4
 + 0
```

4.
```
   4
   1
 + 8
```

5.
```
   983
 − 165
```

6.
```
   841
 − 322
```

7.
```
   629
 − 431
```

8.
```
   739
 − 553
```

Making a List

1. Anne has white bread, rye
bread, turkey, and cheese.
How many different sandwiches
can she make? Make a list to
show the sandwiches.

number of sandwiches ____

Bread	Filling

2. Jim has a white sweater,
a blue sweater, red pants,
and blue pants. How many
different ways can he wear the
sweaters and pants? Make a
list to show the outfits.

number of outfits ____

Sweater	Pants

Review and Remember

Solve by using problem-solving strategies.

1. Jill has 3 cats, 2 dogs, and 2 hamsters.
How many pets does Jill own?

_____

2. Kim invited 8 friends to her party.
Each friend brought 2 gifts.
How many gifts did Kim receive?

_____

Add or subtract.

3.	**4.**	**5.**	**6.**	**7.**
238	542	74	55	96
+ 475	+ 349	− 43	− 9	− 85

Name _____

Reading Graphs

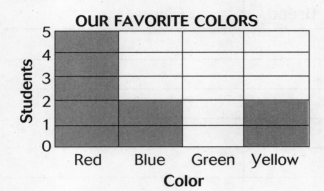

OUR FAVORITE COLORS

Students (y-axis: 0–5), Color (x-axis: Red, Blue, Green, Yellow)

PETS WE HAVE

Fish	✕
Dog	✕ ✕ ✕ ✕ ✕
Cat	✕ ✕ ✕
Bird	✕ ✕

Each ✕ stands for 2 students.

Use the bar graph to answer each question.

1. How many students like yellow best? _____

2. What is the most popular color? _____

3. What is the least popular color? _____

Use the pictograph to answer each question.

4. How many students own dogs? _____

5. What pet do most students have? _____

6. How many students own cats? _____

Review and Remember

Add or subtract.

| **1.** 947 | **2.** 477 | **3.** 888 | **4.** 679 | **5.** 581 |
| + 886 | + 986 | + 347 | + 543 | + 629 |

| **6.** 683 | **7.** 815 | **8.** 783 | **9.** 201 | **10.** 300 |
| + 419 | + 537 | + 927 | − 163 | − 148 |

| **11.** 500 | **12.** 510 | **13.** 709 | **14.** 810 | **15.** 903 |
| − 313 | − 227 | − 247 | − 366 | − 200 |

Using Ordered Pairs to Locate Points

Use the grid to answer each question.

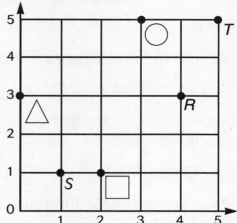

1. What ordered pair gives the location of the square?

_____

2. What ordered pair gives the location of *R*?

_____

3. What ordered pair gives the location of the circle?

_____

4. What ordered pair gives the location of the triangle?

_____

5. What ordered pair gives the location of *S*?

_____

6. What ordered pair gives the location of *T*?

_____

Review and Remember

Add or subtract.

1.	**2.**	**3.**	**4.**
28	72	16	321
31	83	83	− 198
+ 45	+ 9	+ 94	

5.	**6.**	**7.**	**8.**
611	323	227	643
− 294	− 167	− 105	− 271

9. 62 + 47 + 15 _____

10. 17 + 21 + 84 _____

11. 12 + 38 + 92 _____

12. 57 + 22 + 10 _____

Making Graphs

Use the grid.

1. What are the coordinates of point *A*?

_____

2. Locate the following points on the grid and label.

B (6,8) and *C* (3,4)

3. Make up a name for the grid. Write it on top. Connect points *A*, *B*, and *C*.

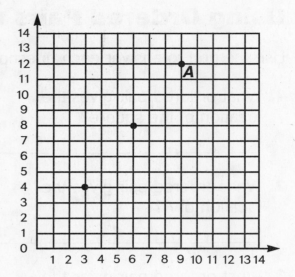

Use the bar graph.

4. Complete the graph to show that 7 students chose chicken nuggets as their favorite lunch.

5. Which lunch did 4 students choose as their favorite?

_____

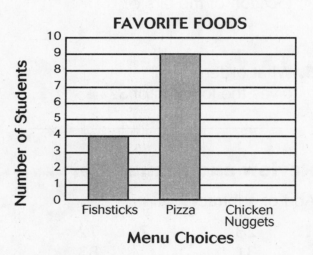

FAVORITE FOODS

Number of Students

Fishsticks   Pizza   Chicken Nuggets

Menu Choices

Review and Remember

Solve.

1. Jan had 1 liter of milk. She used 300 milliliters of milk to make muffins. She used 500 milliliters to make pancakes. How much milk was left?

_____

2. Steve hiked 220 meters to the pond and then 595 meters to the lodge. How far did he hike? How much more or less than a kilometer was that?

_____

_____

Exploring Probability

Circle the letter of the correct answer.

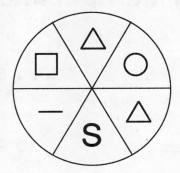

1. The chance of a pointer stopping on □ is?

   a. 1 out of 4

   b. 1 out of 6

   c. 1 out of 3

2. The chance of a pointer stopping on **S** is?

   a. 1 out of 4

   b. 1 out of 6

   c. 2 out of 6

3. The chance of a pointer stopping on △ is?

   a. 1 out of 4

   b. 1 out of 6

   c. 2 out of 6

Use the table to answer each question.

4. How many times did heads show?

_____

5. How many times did tails show?

_____

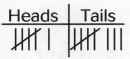

Heads	Tails
IIII I	IIII IIII

6. Why are these results about the same?

_____

Review and Remember

Add, subtract, or multiply.

1.   3
   + 3

2.   4
   + 5

3.   3
   + 6

4.   6
   − 4

5.   4
   − 4

6.   5
   − 3

7.   2
   × 3

8.   2
   × 2

9.   3
   × 3

10.   1
   × 6

11.   4
   × 0

12.   5
   × 1

Relating Multiplication and Division

Multiply or divide.

1. $3 \times 6 =$ _____

$6 \times 3 =$ _____

$18 \div 3 =$ _____

$18 \div 6 =$ _____

2. $2 \times 5 =$ _____

$5 \times 2 =$ _____

$10 \div 2 =$ _____

$10 \div 5 =$ _____

3. $3 \times 4 =$ _____

$4 \times 3 =$ _____

$12 \div 4 =$ _____

$12 \div 3 =$ _____

Multiply. Then write two division sentences.

4. $3 \times 5 =$ _____

$5 \times 3 =$ _____

____ $\div$ ____ $= 5$

____ $\div$ ____ $= 3$

5. $3 \times 7 =$ _____

$7 \times 3 =$ _____

____ $\div$ ____ $= 7$

____ $\div$ ____ $= 3$

6. $2 \times 6 =$ _____

$6 \times 2 =$ _____

____ $\div$ ____ $=$ ____

____ $\div$ ____ $=$ ____

Review and Remember

Choose the correct word to complete each sentence.

gram   **centimeter**   **kilogram**

1. To measure lengths, use the _____.

2. To measure the weight of light objects, use the _____.

3. To measure the weight of heavy objects, use the _____.

Using 2 and 3 as Divisors

Write a division fact for each.
Then write how many are in each group.

1. 8 animals
4 equal groups

2. 9 birds
3 equal groups

_____   _____

Divide.

3. $12 \div 3 =$ _____   **4.** $2 \div 2 =$ _____   **5.** $14 \div 2 =$ _____

6. $18 \div 3 =$ _____   **7.** $12 \div 2 =$ _____   **8.** $27 \div 3 =$ _____

9. $21 \div 3 =$ _____   **10.** $18 \div 2 =$ _____   **11.** $10 \div 2 =$ _____

12. $16 \div 2 =$ _____   **13.** $15 \div 3 =$ _____   **14.** $6 \div 3 =$ _____

15. $2\overline{)6}$ **16.** $3\overline{)24}$ **17.** $3\overline{)18}$ **18.** $3\overline{)27}$

Review and Remember

Add, subtract, or multiply.

1. $\begin{array}{r} 23 \\ + 41 \\ \hline \end{array}$ **2.** $\begin{array}{r} 12 \\ + 23 \\ \hline \end{array}$ **3.** $\begin{array}{r} 16 \\ + 33 \\ \hline \end{array}$ **4.** $\begin{array}{r} 45 \\ + 34 \\ \hline \end{array}$

5. $\begin{array}{r} 35 \\ - 12 \\ \hline \end{array}$ **6.** $\begin{array}{r} 67 \\ - 43 \\ \hline \end{array}$ **7.** $\begin{array}{r} 89 \\ - 25 \\ \hline \end{array}$ **8.** $\begin{array}{r} 93 \\ - 71 \\ \hline \end{array}$

9. $\begin{array}{r} 6 \\ \times 2 \\ \hline \end{array}$ **10.** $\begin{array}{r} 5 \\ \times 3 \\ \hline \end{array}$ **11.** $\begin{array}{r} 8 \\ \times 2 \\ \hline \end{array}$ **12.** $\begin{array}{r} 9 \\ \times 3 \\ \hline \end{array}$

Two-Step Problems

Read each problem and solve.

1. Jean had $5.00. She spent $2.25 in one store and $1.30 in another store. How much money does she have left?

_____

2. Frank, Sal, and Travis were in a 500 m relay race. Frank ran 150 m, Sal ran 175 m. How far did Travis run?

_____

3. Cindy picked 3 bunches of flowers. Each bunch had 6 flowers. She gave 1 bunch of flowers to her mother. How many flowers does Cindy have left?

_____

4. Lisa's sister baby-sat for the Johnsons for 3 hours. She then baby-sat for the Millers for 2 hours. She was paid $2 an hour for baby-sitting. How much money was Lisa's sister paid?

_____

5. Marie read 21 pages in her book before lunch. She read 17 pages after lunch. Tommy read 32 pages after lunch. How many more pages did Marie read than Tommy?

_____

Review and Remember

Solve.

1. Marsha read 175 pages. The book has 202 pages. How many pages does Marsha have left to read?

_____

2. There are 124 pages in a book, 216 in another, and 439 in another. How many pages in all are in the 3 books?

_____

Name _____

Using 4 and 5 as Divisors

Divide.

1. 8 ÷ 4 = _____   **2.** 12 ÷ 4 = _____   **3.** 4 ÷ 4 = _____

4. 16 ÷ 4 = _____   **5.** 10 ÷ 5 = _____   **6.** 25 ÷ 5 = _____

7. 24 ÷ 4 = _____   **8.** 36 ÷ 4 = _____   **9.** 15 ÷ 5 = _____

10. 36 ÷ 4 = _____   **11.** 45 ÷ 5 = _____   **12.** 40 ÷ 5 = _____

Complete. Follow each rule.

Rule: Divide by 5

	Input	Output
13.	5	
14.	10	
15.	15	
16.	20	

Rule: Divide by 4

	Input	Output
17.	4	
18.	12	
19.	16	
20.	28	

Review and Remember

Add, subtract, or multiply.

1. 27
       + 17

2. 15
       + 26

3. 71
       − 19

4. 63
       − 34

5.   7
       × 4

6.   3
       × 4

7.   9
       × 4

8.   6
       × 4

9. 13
       + 27

10. 35
       + 19

11. 84
       − 56

12. 72
       − 39

Using 0 and 1 in Division

Find each quotient.

1. $5 \div 5 =$ _____ **2.** $0 \div 5 =$ _____ **3.** $9 \div 9 =$ _____

4. $6 \div 1 =$ _____ **5.** $8 \div 1 =$ _____ **6.** $2 \div 1 =$ _____

7. $0 \div 3 =$ _____ **8.** $0 \div 5 =$ _____ **9.** $0 \div 7 =$ _____

10. $6 \div 6 =$ _____ **11.** $0 \div 8 =$ _____ **12.** $5 \div 1 =$ _____

13. $4\overline{)0}$ **14.** $7\overline{)7}$ **15.** $1\overline{)3}$ **16.** $4\overline{)4}$

Solve.

17. Vanessa has 6 pictures. She pastes 6 pictures on each poster. How many posters can she make?

_____

18. Mark made 4 birthday cards. He put 1 in each envelope. How many envelopes did he have?

_____

Review and Remember

Add, subtract, or multiply. Use mental math or paper and pencil.

1. $\begin{array}{r} 31 \\ + 82 \\ \hline \end{array}$ **2.** $\begin{array}{r} 71 \\ + 63 \\ \hline \end{array}$ **3.** $\begin{array}{r} 80 \\ + 94 \\ \hline \end{array}$ **4.** $\begin{array}{r} 36 \\ + 72 \\ \hline \end{array}$

5. $\begin{array}{r} 478 \\ - 312 \\ \hline \end{array}$ **6.** $\begin{array}{r} 894 \\ - 123 \\ \hline \end{array}$ **7.** $\begin{array}{r} 675 \\ - 461 \\ \hline \end{array}$ **8.** $\begin{array}{r} 549 \\ - 123 \\ \hline \end{array}$

9. $\begin{array}{r} 8 \\ \times 5 \\ \hline \end{array}$ **10.** $\begin{array}{r} 6 \\ \times 5 \\ \hline \end{array}$ **11.** $\begin{array}{r} 9 \\ \times 5 \\ \hline \end{array}$ **12.** $\begin{array}{r} 3 \\ \times 5 \\ \hline \end{array}$

Dividing by 6

Complete each sentence. Multiply or divide.

1. $6 \times \boxed{} = 24$ **2.** $6 \times \boxed{} = 48$ **3.** $6 \times \boxed{} = 0$ **4.** $6 \times \boxed{} = 18$

$24 \div 6 = \boxed{}$ $48 \div 6 = \boxed{}$ $0 \div 6 = \boxed{}$ $18 \div 6 = \boxed{}$

5. $6 \times \boxed{} = 36$ **6.** $5 \times \boxed{} = 20$ **7.** $6 \times \boxed{} = 12$ **8.** $3 \times \boxed{} = 24$

$36 \div 6 = \boxed{}$ $20 \div 5 = \boxed{}$ $12 \div 6 = \boxed{}$ $24 \div 3 = \boxed{}$

Divide.

9. $6 \overline{)48}$ **10.** $6 \overline{)24}$ **11.** $4 \overline{)36}$ **12.** $6 \overline{)30}$ **13.** $6 \overline{)12}$

14. $6 \overline{)6}$ **15.** $2 \overline{)6}$ **16.** $6 \overline{)42}$ **17.** $3 \overline{)24}$ **18.** $6 \overline{)54}$

19. $3 \overline{)18}$ **20.** $6 \overline{)0}$ **21.** $4 \overline{)32}$ **22.** $6 \overline{)18}$ **23.** $6 \overline{)36}$

24. $48 \div 6 = \boxed{}$ **25.** $6 \div \boxed{} = 1$ **26.** $\boxed{} \div 6 = 4$ **27.** $\boxed{} \div 6 = 3$

28. $54 \div 6 = \boxed{}$ **29.** $18 \div \boxed{} = 3$ **30.** $\boxed{} \div 6 = 7$ **31.** $\boxed{} \div 5 = 6$

32. $12 \div \boxed{} = 2$ **33.** $24 \div \boxed{} = 6$ **34.** $6 \div \boxed{} = 6$ **35.** $\boxed{} \div 6 = 6$

Review and Remember

Add or subtract.

1. $\begin{array}{r} 345 \\ + 534 \\ \hline \end{array}$ **2.** $\begin{array}{r} 198 \\ + 764 \\ \hline \end{array}$ **3.** $\begin{array}{r} 549 \\ + 429 \\ \hline \end{array}$ **4.** $\begin{array}{r} 397 \\ - 218 \\ \hline \end{array}$ **5.** $\begin{array}{r} 617 \\ - 338 \\ \hline \end{array}$ **6.** $\begin{array}{r} 645 \\ - 223 \\ \hline \end{array}$

Using 8 and 9 as Divisors

Find each quotient.

1. $8\overline{)32}$ **2.** $8\overline{)48}$ **3.** $9\overline{)27}$ **4.** $9\overline{)45}$

5. $9\overline{)81}$ **6.** $8\overline{)72}$ **7.** $9\overline{)54}$ **8.** $8\overline{)24}$

9. $8\overline{)0}$ **10.** $8\overline{)40}$ **11.** $9\overline{)18}$ **12.** $9\overline{)63}$

13. $9\overline{)9}$ **14.** $9\overline{)0}$ **15.** $8\overline{)64}$ **16.** $8\overline{)56}$

17. $36 \div 9 =$ ____   **18.** $32 \div 8 =$ ____   **19.** $45 \div 9 =$ ____   **20.** $8 \div 8 =$ ____

21. $24 \div 8 =$ ____   **22.** $27 \div 9 =$ ____   **23.** $9 \div 9 =$ ____   **24.** $18 \div 9 =$ ____

Circle the letter of the correct number sentence. Then solve the problem.

25. There were 48 chairs in the classroom. There were 8 equal rows of chairs. How many chairs were in each row?

     a. $48 + 8 = \square$
     b. $48 - 8 = \square$
     c. $48 \times 8 = \square$
     d. $48 \div 8 = \square$

_____

Review and Remember

Multiply or divide.

1. $6 \times 7 =$ _____   **2.** $4 \times 8 =$ _____   **3.** $7 \times 3 =$ _____

4. $25 \div 5 =$ _____   **5.** $7 \div 7 =$ _____   **6.** $14 \div 2 =$ _____

7. $\begin{array}{r} 6 \\ \times\, 3 \\ \hline \end{array}$ **8.** $\begin{array}{r} 2 \\ \times\, 8 \\ \hline \end{array}$ **9.** $\begin{array}{r} 9 \\ \times\, 7 \\ \hline \end{array}$ **10.** $\begin{array}{r} 7 \\ \times\, 8 \\ \hline \end{array}$

Multiplication and Division Facts

Complete each fact family.

1. $7 \times 2 =$ _____

   $2 \times 7 =$ _____

   $14 \div$ _____ $= 7$

   $14 \div 7 =$ _____

2. $4 \times 3 =$ _____

   $3 \times 4 =$ _____

   _____ $\div 4 = 3$

   _____ $\div 3 = 4$

3. $5 \times 8 =$ _____

   $8 \times 5 =$ _____

   _____ $\div 8 = 5$

   _____ $\div 5 = 8$

Give the other facts in each family.

4. $6 \times 8 = 48$

   _____ $\times$ _____ $=$ _____

   _____ $\div$ _____ $=$ _____

   _____ $\div$ _____ $=$ _____

5. $8 \times 3 = 24$

   _____ $\times$ _____ $=$ _____

   _____ $\div$ _____ $=$ _____

   _____ $\div$ _____ $=$ _____

6. $4 \times 7 = 28$

   _____ $\times$ _____ $=$ _____

   _____ $\div$ _____ $=$ _____

   _____ $\div$ _____ $=$ _____

Find the missing number.

7. $7 \times$ _____ $= 0$

8. $45 \div$ _____ $= 5$

9. _____ $\times 4 = 24$

10. $8 \times$ _____ $= 8$

11. $9 \div$ _____ $= 9$

12. $8 \times$ _____ $= 16$

13. $5 \times$ _____ $= 25$

14. $24 \div$ _____ $= 6$

15. _____ $\times 3 = 15$

16. $3 \times$ _____ $= 6$

17. _____ $\div 2 = 9$

18. $4 \times$ _____ $= 12$

Review and Remember

Add or subtract.

1. $\begin{array}{r} 87 \\ + 53 \\ \hline \end{array}$

2. $\begin{array}{r} 97 \\ + 66 \\ \hline \end{array}$

3. $\begin{array}{r} 67 \\ + 54 \\ \hline \end{array}$

4. $\begin{array}{r} 87 \\ + 49 \\ \hline \end{array}$

5. $\begin{array}{r} 317 \\ - 125 \\ \hline \end{array}$

6. $\begin{array}{r} 252 \\ - 161 \\ \hline \end{array}$

7. $\begin{array}{r} 348 \\ - 119 \\ \hline \end{array}$

8. $\begin{array}{r} 246 \\ - 158 \\ \hline \end{array}$

Name _____

Division Practice

Divide.

1. $2\overline{)14}$ **2.** $2\overline{)18}$ **3.** $3\overline{)24}$ **4.** $3\overline{)22}$ **5.** $4\overline{)20}$ **6.** $4\overline{)32}$

7. $5\overline{)35}$ **8.** $5\overline{)45}$ **9.** $6\overline{)0}$ **10.** $7\overline{)0}$ **11.** $1\overline{)9}$ **12.** $1\overline{)3}$

13. $6\overline{)24}$ **14.** $6\overline{)54}$ **15.** $6\overline{)19}$ **16.** $7\overline{)49}$ **17.** $7\overline{)42}$ **18.** $7\overline{)63}$

Complete each fact family.

19. $7 \times 5 = 35$ **20.** $8 \times 6 = 48$ **21.** $9 \times 8 = 72$

___ × ___ = ___   ___ × ___ = ___   ___ × ___ = ___

___ ÷ ___ = ___   ___ ÷ ___ = ___   ___ ÷ ___ = ___

___ ÷ ___ = ___   ___ ÷ ___ = ___   ___ ÷ ___ = ___

22. $6 \times 4 = 24$ **23.** $6 \times 7 = 42$ **24.** $8 \times 5 = 40$

___ × ___ = ___   ___ × ___ = ___   ___ × ___ = ___

___ ÷ ___ = ___   ___ ÷ ___ = ___   ___ ÷ ___ = ___

___ ÷ ___ = ___   ___ ÷ ___ = ___   ___ ÷ ___ = ___

Review and Remember

Add or subtract.

1. $\begin{array}{r} 341 \\ + 232 \\ \hline \end{array}$ **2.** $\begin{array}{r} 172 \\ + 413 \\ \hline \end{array}$ **3.** $\begin{array}{r} 300 \\ + 161 \\ \hline \end{array}$ **4.** $\begin{array}{r} 401 \\ + 183 \\ \hline \end{array}$

5. $\begin{array}{r} 310 \\ - 140 \\ \hline \end{array}$ **6.** $\begin{array}{r} 701 \\ - 451 \\ \hline \end{array}$ **7.** $\begin{array}{r} 600 \\ - 361 \\ \hline \end{array}$ **8.** $\begin{array}{r} 810 \\ - 643 \\ \hline \end{array}$

Name _____

Using Operations

Library	
Opens 7:50 A.M.	
Closes 3:45 P.M.	
Return books by 3:30 P.M.	

Bookstore
Opens 8:00 A.M.
Closes 4:00 P.M.

Math book	$3.95
Science book	$3.95
Notebook	$0.39
Pencil	$0.25
Pen	$0.17

Cross out any extra information. Use the signs to solve.

1. Connie has $5. Can she buy a new math book and a pencil? _____

2. Jeremy arrived at school at 7:45 A.M. How long will he have to wait for the library to open? _____

3. Mrs. Petrie works in the bookstore from the time it opens until it closes. Miss Galen works in the cafeteria. How long does Mrs. Petrie work each day if she has a 30 minute lunch? _____

4. Timmy had 60¢. He bought 2 items at the bookstore. What items could he buy? _____

_____

5. Emily begins putting books on the shelves at 3:30. Emily can put 2 books on shelves every minute. How many books will Emily put on the shelves by the time the library closes? _____

Review and Remember

Multiply.

1. 8	**2.** 5	**3.** 4	**4.** 9	**5.** 7	**6.** 6
× 4	× 7	× 3	× 8	× 6	× 3

7. $0 \times 5 =$ _____   **8.** $5 \times 9 =$ _____   **9.** $6 \times 6 =$ _____

Name Plane Figures

Name each plane figure.

1.   _____

2.   _____

3.   _____

4.  _____

5. Which figure has no straight sides and no corners? _____

6. Which figure has 3 sides and 3 corners? _____

7. Which figure has 4 equal sides? _____

8. Which figure has 2 pairs of equal sides? _____

Name the first figure. Circle the letters of the same kind of figure.

9.   a.    b.   c.   d.

_____

10.   a.   b.   c.   d.

_____

Review and Remember

Add or subtract.

1.   234
  + 165
	2. 420
	  + 389
		3. 754
		  + 208
			4. 733
			  + 198

5.   641
  − 339
	6. 800
	  − 528
		7. 529
		  − 311
			8. 402
			  − 230

Name _____

Lines, Line Segments, Rays, and Right Angles

Name each figure.

1.   **2.**   **3.**   **4.**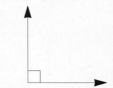

_____   _____   _____   _____

Name the line segments in each figure.

5.    **6.** 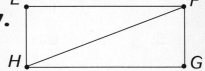   **7.**

_____   _____   _____

Name the first figure. Circle the letters of the same kind of figure.

8.   **a.**   **b.**   **c.**   **d.**

_____

9.   **a.**   **b.**   **c.**    **d.**

_____

Review and Remember
Add or subtract.

1. 27
      + 16

2. 35
      + 36

3. 49
      + 28

4. 84
      − 18

5. 62
      − 39

Naming Congruent and Symmetric Figures

Are the figures in each pair congruent? Write *yes* or *no*.

1. 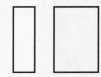   **2.**    **3.**   **4.**

_____   _____   _____   _____

Find the figures in each row that are congruent to the first figure in the row.

5.   **a.**   **b.**   **c.**   **d.**

6.   **a.**   **b.**   **c.**   **d.**

Is the dashed line a line of symmetry? Write *yes* or *no*.

7.   **8.**   **9.**   **10.**

_____   _____   _____   _____

Review and Remember

Add, subtract, multiply, or divide.

1.   923
  − 378

2.   678
  + 244

3.   2,605
  − 1,206

4.   5,239
  + 4,181

5. $3 \times 6 = $ _____   **6.** $9 \times 3 = $ _____   **7.** $36 \div 6 = $ _____   **8.** $28 \div 7 = $ _____

Name _____

Finding Perimeter and Area

Find the perimeter of each figure.

1.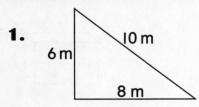

6 m 10 m 8 m

_____

2. 4 cm 5 cm 5 cm 4 cm

_____

3.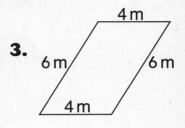

4 m 6 m 6 m 4 m

_____

Find the area of each figure.

4.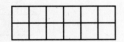

_____

5.

_____

6.

_____

7.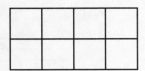

_____

8.

_____

9.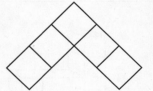

_____

Review and Remember

Add, subtract, multiply, or divide.

1.   89
      + 76

2.   47
      + 83

3.   66
      + 74

4. 329
     − 144

5.   682
      − 234

6.   417
      − 132

7.   7
       × 4

8.   3
        × 4

9. $8\overline{)16}$

10. $4\overline{)24}$

11. $8\overline{)40}$

12. $5\overline{)35}$

Use after Grade 3, text page 383. **49**

Volume

Find the volume of each figure.

1.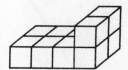

_____

2.

_____

3.

_____

4.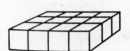

_____

5.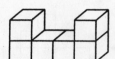

_____

6.

_____

7.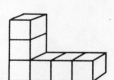

_____

8.

_____

9.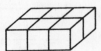

_____

Review and Remember

Write the time.

1. It is 12:15 P.M. Lunch starts in 15 minutes. What time does lunch start?

_____

2. It is 11:30 A.M. What time will it be in 1 hour and 40 minutes?

_____

Add, subtract, divide, or multiply.

3. 465
− 278

4. 53
+ 79

5. 8)65

6. 7
× 7

Naming Equivalent Fractions

Use what you know about equivalent fractions
to find each missing number.

1.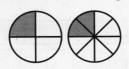

$$\frac{1}{4} = \frac{\Box}{8}$$

2.

$$\frac{2}{5} = \frac{4}{\Box\Box}$$

3.

$$\frac{2}{3} = \frac{\Box}{\Box}$$

4.

$$\frac{1}{2} = \frac{\Box}{4}$$

5.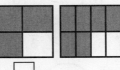

$$\frac{3}{4} = \frac{\Box}{8}$$

6.

$$\frac{1}{3} = \frac{\Box}{6}$$

7.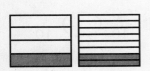

$$\frac{1}{4} = \frac{\Box}{\Box}$$

8.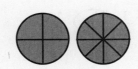

$$\frac{4}{4} = \frac{\Box}{\Box}$$

9.

$$\frac{3}{3} = \frac{\Box}{\Box}$$

Circle the letter of the greater amount.

10.

a. $\frac{1}{4}$ of the muffins

b. $\frac{1}{3}$ of the muffins

Review and Remember

Multiply or divide.

1.
$$\begin{array}{r} 8 \\ \times 9 \\ \hline \end{array}$$

2.
$$\begin{array}{r} 9 \\ \times 7 \\ \hline \end{array}$$

3.
$$\begin{array}{r} 6 \\ \times 4 \\ \hline \end{array}$$

4.
$$\begin{array}{r} 6 \\ \times 2 \\ \hline \end{array}$$

5. $5\overline{)35}$

6. $8\overline{)24}$

Name _____

Comparing Fractions

Compare. Write >, <, or = in each ⬭.
Use fraction pieces if you like.

1.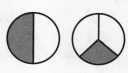

$\frac{1}{2}$ ⬭ $\frac{1}{3}$

2.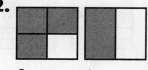

$\frac{3}{4}$ ⬭ $\frac{1}{2}$

3.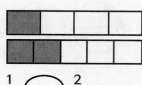

$\frac{1}{4}$ ⬭ $\frac{2}{5}$

4. $\frac{4}{10}$ ⬭ $\frac{4}{10}$

5. $\frac{7}{10}$ ⬭ $\frac{3}{10}$

6. $\frac{2}{10}$ ⬭ $\frac{9}{10}$

7. $\frac{2}{8}$ ⬭ $\frac{5}{8}$

8. $\frac{1}{6}$ ⬭ $\frac{1}{3}$

9. $\frac{4}{8}$ ⬭ $\frac{1}{2}$

10. $\frac{1}{5}$ ⬭ $\frac{1}{6}$

11. $\frac{3}{5}$ ⬭ $\frac{3}{4}$

12. $\frac{6}{8}$ ⬭ $\frac{3}{4}$

13. $\frac{4}{10}$ ⬭ $\frac{2}{5}$

14. $\frac{5}{8}$ ⬭ $\frac{7}{8}$

15. $\frac{3}{6}$ ⬭ $\frac{1}{3}$

16. $\frac{1}{5}$ ⬭ $\frac{3}{4}$

17. $\frac{3}{4}$ ⬭ $\frac{1}{4}$

18. $\frac{3}{10}$ ⬭ $\frac{9}{10}$

Solve.

19. Jan used $\frac{1}{3}$ of a can of paint. Terry used $\frac{3}{8}$ of a can. Who used more paint?

_____

20. Diane's glass of juice is $\frac{2}{3}$ full. Peter's glass is $\frac{1}{2}$ full. Whose glass has more juice in it?

_____

Review and Remember

Multiply or divide.

1. $\begin{array}{r} 4 \\ \times\ 5 \\ \hline \end{array}$

2. $\begin{array}{r} 6 \\ \times\ 8 \\ \hline \end{array}$

3. $7\overline{)28}$

4. $5\overline{)35}$

5. $6\overline{)36}$

Finding Fractional Parts

Complete.

1. $\frac{1}{2}$ of 6 = _____

2. $\frac{1}{3}$ of 9 = _____

3. $\frac{1}{2}$ of 2 = _____

4. $\frac{1}{8}$ of 64 = _____

5. $\frac{1}{5}$ of 10 = _____

6. $\frac{1}{9}$ of 81 = _____

7. $\frac{1}{7}$ of 21 = _____

8. $\frac{1}{4}$ of 24 = _____

9. $\frac{1}{6}$ of 18 = _____

10. $\frac{1}{8}$ of 56 = _____

11. $\frac{1}{2}$ of 14 = _____

12. $\frac{1}{3}$ of 24 = _____

13. $\frac{1}{6}$ of 30 = _____

14. $\frac{1}{5}$ of 25 = _____

15. $\frac{1}{7}$ of 49 = _____

16. $\frac{1}{4}$ of 32 = _____

17. $\frac{1}{2}$ of 18 = _____

18. $\frac{1}{6}$ of 6 = _____

Solve.

19. There are 72 students in the band and $\frac{1}{9}$ of them are third-graders. How many students are third-graders?

_____

20. Fourth-graders make up $\frac{1}{8}$ of the band. How many students are fourth-graders?

_____

Review and Remember

Multiply, divide, or add.

1. 7
   $\times\ 3$

2. 8
   $\times\ 5$

3. 6
   $\times\ 0$

4. 5
   $\times\ 3$

5. 1
   $\times\ 8$

6. $7\overline{)49}$

7. $8\overline{)24}$

8. $4\overline{)16}$

9. $8\overline{)40}$

10. $9\overline{)63}$

11. 24 + 69 + 33 _____

12. 15 + 92 + 47 _____

Decimals in Hundredths

Choose the greater number. Circle your answer.

1. 0.25 or 0.52   **2.** 0.81 or 0.78   **3.** 0.47 or 0.27

4. 0.12 or 0.02   **5.** 0.09 or 0.08   **6.** 0.34 or 0.43

Choose two of the numbers 2, 5, or 7 to write a decimal:

7. less than 0.33. _____   **8.** less than 0.75. _____

9. greater than 0.5. _____   **10.** greater than 0.6. _____

Compare. Write >, <, or = in each $\bigcirc$.

11. 0.03 $\bigcirc$ 0.30   **12.** 0.12 $\bigcirc$ 0.10   **13.** 0.67 $\bigcirc$ 0.67

14. 0.46 $\bigcirc$ 0.45   **15.** 0.32 $\bigcirc$ 0.09   **16.** 0.27 $\bigcirc$ 0.72

17. 0.2 $\bigcirc$ 0.20   **18.** 0.91 $\bigcirc$ 0.92   **19.** 0.32 $\bigcirc$ 0.82

20. thirty hundredths $\bigcirc$ three tenths

Review and Remember

Add, subtract, multiply, or divide. Use mental math or paper and pencil.

1.   0
   + 2

2.   23
   − 0

3.   173
   + 569

4.   432
   − 308

5.   486
   − 80

6.   9,753
   − 5,602

7.   8,329
   − 5,328

8.   589
   − 193

9.   9
   × 4

10.   7
   × 8

11.   32
   − 27

12. 3$\overline{)27}$

13.   401
   + 516

14.   6
   × 7

15. 8$\overline{)48}$

Name _____

Reading and Writing Decimals Greater Than 1

Write a decimal for the shaded part.

1.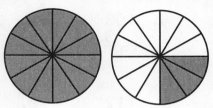

_____

2.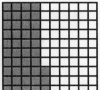

_____

Write each as a decimal.

3. $3\frac{2}{100}$ _____

4. $7\frac{9}{10}$ _____

5. $4\frac{4}{10}$ _____

6. nine and twenty-seven hundredths _____

7. four and five hundredths _____

8. eight and six tenths _____

9. three and twelve hundredths _____

Write in words. Name the value of the digit 3.

10. 7.13 _____

11. 4.39 _____

Choose the greater number. Circle your answer.

12. 9.4 or 9.42   **13.** 4.29 or 4.30   **14.** 5.27 or 5.17

Review and Remember

Add or subtract.
Use mental math or pencil and paper.

1.	**2.**	**3.**	**4.**	**5.**
39	83	$ 0.18	69	88
76	59	0.09	7	− 79
+ 2	+ 4	+ 0.35	+ 80	

          Use after Grade 3, text page 427.

Multiplying Three-Digit Numbers

Multiply.

1. 222 × 4	**2.** 142 × 2	**3.** 101 × 8	**4.** 103 × 3	**5.** 210 × 3
6. 105 × 8	**7.** 106 × 9	**8.** 108 × 7	**9.** 112 × 7	**10.** 115 × 5
11. 120 × 6	**12.** 121 × 6	**13.** 140 × 5	**14.** 141 × 5	**15.** 162 × 4
16. 412 × 6	**17.** 500 × 6	**18.** 580 × 4	**19.** 900 × 9	**20.** 400 × 7
21. 401 × 4	**22.** 517 × 5	**23.** 327 × 3	**24.** 202 × 8	**25.** 900 × 0

Review and Remember

Name each figure.

1. four equal straight sides _____

2. no straight sides and no corners _____

3. three straight sides and three corners _____

4.

5.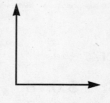

6.

_____   _____   _____

Name _____

Multiplying Greater Numbers

Circle the better estimate.

1. 409 × 6

240 or 2,400

2. 598 × 7

3,500 or 4,200

3. 920 × 5

4,500 or 5,300

Estimate. Then find each product.

4.   615
   × 7

5.   921
   × 8

6.   785
   × 7

7.   510
   × 6

8.   499
   × 5

9.   509
   × 7

10.   514
    × 6

11.   620
    × 8

12.   732
    × 3

13.   715
    × 9

14.   681
    × 6

15.   823
    × 8

Review and Remember

Find the perimeter of each figure.

1.

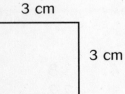

3 cm

3 cm

2.

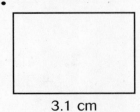

2.7 cm

3.1 cm

3.

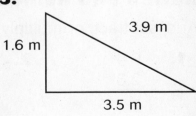

3.9 m

1.6 m

3.5 m

_____

_____

_____

Estimating Products

Estimate each product.

1. 72
    $\times\ 3$

2. 38
    $\times\ 4$

3. 93
    $\times\ 7$

4. 66
    $\times\ 3$

5. 377
    $\times\ \ 6$

6. 213
    $\times\ \ 8$

7. 623
    $\times\ \ 2$

8. 782
    $\times\ \ 7$

9. 7×78 _____

10. 5×495 _____

11. 3×828 _____

Estimate. Write $>$, $<$, or $=$ in each $\bigcirc$.

12. $7 \times 38 \bigcirc 300$

13. $40 \times 6 \bigcirc 8 \times 30$

14. $6 \times 71 \bigcirc 49 \times 8$

15. $120 \times 7 \bigcirc 2 \times 308$

Use estimation to solve.

16. Lorna is making jewelry. Each necklace has 8 beads. About how many beads does she need to make 27 necklaces?

_____beads

17. Theo has 23 math problems for homework each night. About how many problems does he have in 7 nights?

_____problems

Review and Remember

Add, subtract, or multiply.

1. 6.4
    $+\ 2.8$

2. 2.4
    $-\ 1.5$

3. 4.7
    $+\ 3.7$

4. 3.8
    $-\ 2.2$

5. 8
    $\times 6$

6. 5
    $\times 7$

7. 6
    $\times 4$

8. 12
    $\times\ 0$

Using Remainders

Find each quotient.

1. $2\overline{)16}$ **2.** $5\overline{)18}$ **3.** $4\overline{)29}$ **4.** $5\overline{)27}$

5. $6\overline{)62}$ **6.** $5\overline{)60}$ **7.** $5\overline{)86}$ **8.** $4\overline{)87}$

9. $78 \div 7$ _____   **10.** $84 \div 9$ _____   **11.** $72 \div 8$ _____

12. $76 \div 5$ _____   **13.** $95 \div 3$ _____   **14.** $87 \div 2$ _____

Compare. Write $>$, $<$, or $=$ in each $\bigcirc$.

15. $90 \div 3 \bigcirc 90 \div 4$ **16.** $38 \div 4 \bigcirc 29 \div 3$

17. $96 \div 3 \bigcirc 16 \times 2$ **18.** $47 \div 6 \bigcirc 53 \div 8$

19. $31 \div 3 \bigcirc 43 \div 4$ **20.** $50 \div 7 \bigcirc 60 \div 8$

Review and Remember

Add, subtract, multiply, or divide.
Use mental math or paper and pencil.

1. $\begin{array}{r} 378 \\ + 287 \end{array}$ **2.** $\begin{array}{r} 429 \\ - 197 \end{array}$ **3.** $\begin{array}{r} 335 \\ + 479 \end{array}$ **4.** $\begin{array}{r} 8,674 \\ - 3,012 \end{array}$ **5.** $\begin{array}{r} 72 \\ \times\ \ 6 \end{array}$

6. $\begin{array}{r} 937 \\ - 258 \end{array}$ **7.** $\begin{array}{r} 682 \\ + 357 \end{array}$ **8.** $\begin{array}{r} 504 \\ - 375 \end{array}$ **9.** $\begin{array}{r} 5,682 \\ + 3,241 \end{array}$ **10.** $\begin{array}{r} 59 \\ \times\ \ 5 \end{array}$

11. 210×0 _____   **12.** $9\overline{)0}$ **13.** $6\overline{)48}$ **14.** $49 \div 7$ _____

      Use after Grade 3, text page 463.

Division Patterns

Use patterns to divide.

1. 2)4   2)40   2)400   **2.** 4)24   4)240   4)2,400

3. 5)35   5)350   5)3,500   **4.** 7)21   7)210   7)2,100

5. 3)27   3)270   3)2,700   **6.** 6)30   6)300   6)3,000

7. 3)900   **8.** 8)3,200   **9.** 6)4,800

10. 350 ÷ 5 _____   **11.** 1,500 ÷ 3 _____   **12.** 1,600 ÷ 8 _____

Find each missing number.

13. 8 ÷ _____ = 1   **14.** 80 ÷ _____ = 10   **15.** 800 ÷ _____ = 100

Solve.

16. There are 60 third graders in Park School. There are the same number of students in each of the 3 classrooms. How many third graders are in each room?

_____ third graders

17. There are 150 dirty desks. Five students offer to wash them. How many desks will each student wash if each student washes the same number of desks?

_____ desks

Review and Remember

Find the volume of each figure.

1.

2.

3.

_____   _____   _____